Alice's Adventures in Wonderland and *Through the Looking Glass*: A Victorian Satire?

Elissa Bradley

Published 2008 by arima publishing

www.arimapublishing.com

ISBN 978 1 84549 319 6

© Elissa Bradley 2008

All rights reserved

This book is copyright. Subject to statutory exception and to provisions of relevant collective licensing agreements, no part of this publication may be reproduced, stored in a retrieval system, or transmitted in any form or by any means, without the prior written permission of the author.

Printed and bound in the United Kingdom

Typeset in Palatino Linotype 12/14

This book is sold subject to the conditions that it shall not, by way of trade or otherwise, be lent, re-sold, hired out, or otherwise circulated without the publisher's prior consent in any form of binding or cover other than that which it is published and without a similar condition including this condition being imposed on the subsequent purchaser.

In this work of fiction, the characters, places and events are either the product of the author's imagination or they are used entirely fictitiously. Any resemblance to actual persons, living or dead, is purely coincidental.

Abramis is an imprint of arima publishing

www.abramis.co.uk

arima publishing
ASK House, Northgate Avenue
Bury St Edmunds, Suffolk IP32 6BB
t: (+44) 01284 700321
www.arimapublishing.com

Acknowledgments

This book is dedicated to those, who without, I would not have achieved any of the things I have to be proud of.

To my Mom and Dad, who planted seeds so that flowers could blossom on my side of the path.

To my brother, Aiden, I can never show you enough what a difference you make.

To my husband, Clint, for always being there, and never being disappointed.

Contents

Introduction 7

Chapter 1: The Mirroring of Carroll's Fears and Doubts 9

Chapter 2: How Carroll is Subversive and Satirizes Victorian Reality 21

Chapter 3: Carroll's Issue 41

Chapter 4: Carroll's Use of Language 55

Conclusion 71

Notes 73

Bibliography 81

Introduction

In 1952 C.S. Lewis Carroll pointed out that the reason for writing a children's book should be 'because a children's story is the best art-form for something you have to say'.[1]

Chapter 1: The Mirroring of Carroll's Fears and Doubts

Alice's Adventures in Wonderland tells the story of a young girl who falls down a rabbit hole into a world a chaos and nonsense, during which she shrinks to a size so small that she risks drowning in her own tears, then contrastingly grows so big that she finds herself trapped in the White Rabbit's house and has to be rescued by a Lizard named Bill! Alice attends the Mad Hatter's tea-party, stands trial before a jury compromising of a pack of cards, and plays croquet with the Queen who is most concerned with chopping off everybody's head! Her adventures are made up of many illogical encounters and incidents, such as conversing with the Cheshire Cat, entering a house where the Duchess is being abused by the cook, and taking advice from a caterpillar smoking a hoodkah! However the nonsensical mottos of Wonderland become infuriating to Alice and in an outburst of rage she ends her adventure and wakes up on the riverbank where it all began. In it's sequel, *Through the Looking Glass and What Alice Found There*, Alice becomes a pawn in a huge game of chess and travels across the chessboard in a race to be crowned Queen. Among many more nonsensical conversations and encounters with the strange Wonderland creatures, Alice meets The White Knight and his array of inventions, witnesses the battle of TweedleDee and TweedleDum and is introduced to Humpty Dumpty's strange philosophy of language, before final rejecting the chaos of Wonderland once again in a violent outburst at the Queens' dinner party and waking from what must have been nothing but a curious dream.

Charles Lutwidge Dodgson (Lewis Carroll) told the fairytale of *Alice's Adventures in Wonderland* to the three young daughters of Dean Liddell on 4 July 1862. His friend Robinson Duckworth, Fellow of Trinity, who had assisted him that day in taking the Liddell girls up the Thames from Oxford to Godstow for tea, recorded in his *Diary* that:

> The story was actually composed and spoken *over my shoulder* for the benefit of Alice Liddell. [He rowed stroke and Dodgson rowed bow]. I remember turning round and saying: 'Dodgson, is this an extempory romance of yours?' And he replied: 'Yes, I'm inventing as we go along.' I also remember how, when we had conducted the three children back to the Deanery, Alice said, as she bade us goodnight,

Chapter 1: The Mirroring of Carroll's Fears and Doubts

'Oh Mr. Dodgson, I wish you would write out Alice's Adventures for me!' He said he would try, and he afterwards told me that he sat up nearly the whole night, committing to a M.S. book his recollections of the drolleries with which he had enlivened the afternoon. [2]

The first written manuscript of the story was finished in February 1863 and went on to be published in November 1865. In August 1866 Dodgson began considering a sequel, based on the rest of the stories he could remember telling to the Liddell children. The result, *Through the Looking-Glass and What Alice Found There*, was ready for publication in December 1871. [3]

Carroll's love for nonsense apparently developed from his father. When he was just eight years old he received a letter from Archdeacon Dodgson, his father, whilst away in Leeds, which reads:

Then what a bawling & a tearing of hair there will be! Pigs and babies, camels and Butterflies, rolling in the gutter together – old women rushing up chimneys & cows after them – ducks hiding themselves in coffee cups and fat geeses trying to squeeze themselves into pencil cases – at last the Mayor of Leeds will be found in a soup plate covered up with custard & stuck full of almonds to make him look like a sponge cake that he may escape the dreadful destruction of the town. [4]

The Alice books are full of such nonsense. For example the baby turning into a pig, the Mad Hatter trying to squeeze the dormouse into a teapot, the inanimate objects that spontaneously burst into life at any moment! However, as in interpreted by Jackie Wullschlager (1995, p.48), beyond the social comedy of the *Alice* books lies the rich seam of Carroll's fears and doubts, animated by fantasy into paradigmatic characters and adventures. The underlying structure of the stories; the pack of cards in *Alice's Adventures in Wonderland* and the game of chess that Alice becomes a participant in during *Through the Looking Glass*, clearly reflect Carroll's own life which was characterized by a narrow concern for book learning and formal rules, without knowledge or experience of practical matters. As a result of this lifestyle, Carroll evidently found it extremely difficult to accept adulthood on a

Chapter 1: The Mirroring of Carroll's Fears and Doubts

personal level. It seems that this was the case for all of his ten siblings, very few of whom ever married and who remained a close family throughout the duration of their lives. After the death of his father in 1868 his sisters bought a large house in Guildford where they all lived together, and where Carroll often sheltered himself from the wider realms of society. It was here that he died of pneumonia aged sixty-five:

> 'How wonderfully young your brother looks', the doctor is supposed to have said to his sisters after his death. He marked with his contemporary Edward Lear, the beginning of a tradition of English children's writers who were also particular psychological types: boys who could not grow up. [5]

Alice is very much like Carroll, she tries to maintain her values in a world of turmoil and chaos, never quite fitting in with the rest, following a lonely path through life: "Only it is so very lonely in here!' Alice said in a melancholy voice; and, at the thought of her loneliness, two large tears came rolling down her cheeks.' (AA. p. 177). As was written by a student of the Christ

Church in 1868, 'One of my tutors is the man who wrote *Alice in Wonderland*. He looks something like the Hatter, a little like the Cheshire Cat – most like the Gryphon.' [6] Carroll extends this further by creating characters that he knew he could never be, for example he wrote how 'I pictured to myself the Queen of Hearts as a sort of embodiment of ungovernable passion – a blind and aimless Fury'.[7] Jackie Wullschalger (1995, p.49) suggests how Carroll's fear and incomprehension of marriage and sexuality is hinted at in the opening poem of *Through the Looking Glass:*

> Come, hearken then, ere voice of dread,
> With bitter tidings laden,
> Shall summon to unwelcome bed
> A melancholy maiden! (p. 116)

[8]

She discusses further how the gentle sad white pieces who defeat the manic Red Queen play out further his distaste of passion, as he has already informed us how the Red Queen is an embodiment of ungovernable passion.

Chapter 1: The Mirroring of Carroll's Fears and Doubts

For Carroll, passion, lack of control, is associated with intellectual chaos and meaninglessness; much of his life, as an academic logician and as a self-contained bachelor, was about keeping these twin evils at bay. But in the Alice books they have free reign.[9]

A sense of self regret can be captured in the *Alice* books. At the end of *Alice's Adventures in Wonderland,* Alice retells all of her curious adventures to her sister, who then 'dreamed about little Alice herself...and the whole place around her became alive with the strange creatures of her little sisters dream' (AA. p. 110). Carroll's hope and desires are voiced throughout, as 'she [Alice's sister] sat on, with closed eyes, and half believed herself in Wonderland, though she knew she had but to open them again, and all would change to dull reality' (AA. p. 111). Carroll's envy of Alice's virtue, innocence and prospects is clearly mirrored through her sister's narrative:

Lastly, she pictured to herself how this same little sister of hers would, in the after-time, be herself a grown women...and how she would gather about her own children, and make *their* eyes bright and eager with many a strange tale, perhaps even with the dream of Wonderland of long ago...and find pleasure in all their simple joys, remembering her own child-life, and the happy summer days.

(AA. p. 111)

In reality Carroll was restrained by his love for discipline, logic and control. As a result of this he never married or had a family of his own, and his awareness of this is evident in that final paragraph. Carroll wrote to a friend:

So you have been for 12 years, a married man, while I am still a lonely old bachelor! And mean to keep so, for the matter of that. College life is by no means unmixed misery, though married life has no doubt many charms to which I am a stranger. [10]

Through the Looking Glass clearly reflects Carroll's acceptance of his unhappiness. He wrote the sequel to *Alice's Adventures in Wonderland* of his own accord rather than at the request of anybody else, which suggests it was written out of his own needs. Carroll's envy of those around him is voiced throughout:

> 'I wish I could manage to be glad!' the Queen said. 'Only I can never remember the rule. You must be very happy, living in this wood, and being glad whenever you like!'
>
> (AA. p. 177)

Carroll's sheltered lifestyle which was governed by strict logic and discipline perhaps caused him to lose sight of what is truly important in life – happiness. Carroll has forgotten how to be glad.

The character of the White Knight in *Through the Looking Glass* also resembles Carroll, in many respects. 'He is a crazy inventor of games and gadgets ('It's my own invention'), he has a topsy-turvy view of the world and he believes in matters of the mind rather than the body.' [11]:

> 'What does it matter where my body happens to be?' he said. 'My mind goes on working all the same. In fact, the more head-downwards I am, the more I keep inventing new things.'

Alice's Adventures in Wonderland and Through the Looking Glass: A Victorian Satire?

(AA. p. 216)

It almost as though Carroll is trying to justify his life choices, by emphasising the positive side to his lifestyle – 'the more I keep inventing new things', rather than saying 'the more lonely I become'. Posing the question 'What does it matter', also prompts the reader to think about why it does matter, therefore almost mocks the values that Carroll upholds himself, which is perhaps further suggestive of his feelings of regret. The White Knight is one of the few characters who greet Alice with goodwill rather than bitterness or ridicule. He tries his best to amuse her, impressing her with his inventions, singing to her and begging for her sympathy (Chapter 8), but while his song 'of all the strange things that Alice saw in her journey Through the Looking Glass…was the one she remembered most clearly' (AA. p. 218), he knew he could not court her on her way to becoming a Queen, only point her in the right direction:

'You've only a few yards to go,' he said, 'down the hill and over that little brook, and then you'll be a Queen – But you'll stay and see me off first?…I sha'n't be long. You'll wait and wave your hankerchief when I get to that turn in the road? I think it'll encourage me, you see.'

(AA. p.222)

The suggestiveness of the stories that Carroll entertained the Liddell girls with perhaps served to point them in the right direction of life, alongside the influence of his inventions and his love for play, however as is perceived by Jackie Wullschlager (1995) he knew, pathetically, that he was unable to accompany them into adulthood,[12] for he himself was yet to achieve such status. A.L. Taylor titles his biography *The White Knight: A Study of C.L. Dodgson* (Edinburgh, London, 1952), which is strongly suggestive of the notion that the White Knight is a self-portrait by Carroll.

Although the Alice stories were intended to be heard only by three little girls, many attempts have been made to prove that Alice is not simply a children's book, but a carefully constructed allegory ridiculing the political and religious controversies of the day (Ettleson, 1966).[13] Does Lewis to some extent use the *Alice* stories to blame and satire the restraints of the nineteenth century for his inability to accept adulthood; his isolation; and his unhappiness?

Further in depth analysis reveals how Carroll's use of symbolism, language and allusions mirror and mock nineteenth century norms and values, such as; the theories of evolution that were accepted across the political spectrum and the contradicting stance of these in relation to religion; the restrictiveness of the Victorian education system; the failings of contemporary grammarians and faults of literary critics; and the smug narrow mindedness of Victorian society.

Chapter 2: How Carroll is Subversive and Satirizes Victorian Reality

As is defined by Jean-Jacques Lecercle (1994); in classic Marxist terms, nonsense fulfils an ideological function.[14] Through the nonsense of the *Alice* books, Carroll responded to the turbulent period in history in which he lived; the Victorian-era.

Jackie Wullschlager (1995) interprets the Red Queen and the chess pieces featured in *Through the Looking Glass* who find them selves running faster and faster only to stay in the same place as symbolic of the maniacal, ambitious capitalist in new industrial England.[15] Similarly the train in *Through the Looking Glass* reflects Victorian terror at the prospect of powerful new steam engines: "The man that drives the engine. Why, the smoke alone is worth a thousand pounds a puff!" (AA. p. 149). 'In the nonsense of the Alice books, Carroll distilled trends and characteristics which were part of everyday life'.[16] The Victorian period was the great age of Taxonomy, which meant that Victorians were, like the White Queen, expected to believe 'as many as six impossible things before breakfast' (AA. p. 177). There was always news of recent or pending inventions being published, which is reflected in the White Knight in *Through the Looking Glass* who is the embodiment of useless inventions:

> 'I see you're admiring my little box,' the Knight said in a friendly tone. 'It's my own invention – to keep clothes and sandwiches in. You see I carry it upside-down, so that the rain can't get in.'
> 'But the things can get *out*,' Alice gently remarked. 'Do you know the lid's open?'
> 'I didn't know it,' the Knight said, a shade of vexation passing over his face. 'Then all the things must have fallen out! And the box is no use without them.'
>
> (AA. p. 211)

Carroll's techniques function to make the reader become active in their perception of the fairy tale; therefore the medium becomes the text's message. Recognisable proverbs and sayings are reborn through the Duchess's maxims, for example when she adds the moral 'Take care of the sense, and the sounds will take care of themselves' (AA. p. 80) which prompts

Chapter 2: How Carroll is Subversive and Satirizes Victorian Reality

remembrance of the saying 'Take care of the pennies, and the pounds will take care of themselves'. Moralizing nursery rhymes are re-invented as rhymes promoting roughness, such as the 'Speak roughly to your little boy' poem (AA. p. 54) which parodies David Bates (1848) 'Speak Gently'. The narrator's comments whereby he places himself in the text to voice his opinion on matters prompt a meta-textual interpretation of the story. Carroll's use of illustrations and typography also prompt a meta-textual interpretation of the text, for example the Mouse's '…long and sad tale!' (AA. p. 28) where the words are laid out on the page to create the shape of a tail, which is what Alice interprets the word to mean, therefore makes the reader notice the use and function of language. 'Riddles, jokes, and puns also direct the reader's attention to the language, to its potential for semantic duplicity.'[17] Carroll's techniques function to create an edifying world of Victorian fairy tale which parodies the genre.

The nonsense of the *Alice* books ruins the values of Victorian education. In Chapter 2 of *Alice's Adventures in Wonderland* Alice ponders over the correct way to address a mouse:

'O mouse, do you know the right way out of this pool?'…(Alice thought this might be the right way of speaking to a mouse: she had never done such a thing before, but she remembered having seen, in her brother's Latin grammer, 'A mouse – of a mouse – to a mouse – a mouse – O mouse!'

(AA. p. 21)

Within education in Victorian Britain, children were forced to utter unnecessary language items such as the vocative case. As is discussed by Jean-Jacques Lecercle (1994), the vocative 'is the emblem of both the fundamental absurdity of rules of grammar' and the inclusion of the translation of the vocative case provides sarcastic justification (I must learn about vocatives because I may need to address a mouse correctly one day) for the function of such knowledge to feature in daily school life.[18] The uselessness of the vocative case is evident in the fact that it has being lost by most modern languages, therefore this aspect of Carroll's satire was not without motive.

In Chapter 3 of *Alice's Adventures in Wonderland* after swimming around in Alice's unfortunate pool of tears, in an attempt to dry off the Wonderland creatures the mouse sits them down to tell them a story. He amusingly recites:

> "William the Conqueror, whose cause was favoured by the pope, was soon submitted to by the English, who wanted leaders, and had been of late much accustomed to usurpation and conquest. Edwin and Morcar – the earls of Mercia and Northumbria – "
>
> (AA. p. 25)

The story, which the mouse describes as being 'the driest thing I know' (AA. p. 25) is actually quoted from Havilland Chepmell's "Short Course of History" (1862, pp. 143-144); a textbook used by the Liddell children in their lessons. Therefore Carroll is mimicking and mocking the content of Victorian education, perhaps because he blames the dullness of educational material for his failure with students and pupils as a lecturer. In the nineteenth century children were made to learn erratic quotes and excerpts 'without rhyme or reason', all of which would have been as ridiculously incongruous to a Victorian child as Carroll's text of nonsense seems to us. For example the rhyme about Tweedledee and Tweedledum (AA. p. 160) and the other various poems that Alice encounters during her adventures in Wonderland, were probably recited by Carroll from memory. Therefore the inclusion of such within the *Alice* books exposes an education system that is restrictive.

A significant occurrence in *Alice Adventures in Wonderland* with regards to the satire debate is the request by the Caterpillar for Alice to 'Repeat "You are old, Father William," (AA. p. 42). The poem is a parody of Robert Southey's *The Old Man's Comforts* (1799) and was one of the many well-know poems that Victorian children had to learn. Alice recites the poem wrong, therefore the whole value system is, as Father William (in the illustration), turned upside down. One of the stanzas reads:

> 'In my youth,' said his father, 'I took to the law,
> And argued each case with my wife;
> And the muscular strength, which it gave to my jaw
> Has lasted the rest of my life.'
>
> (AA. p.44)

It is questionable whether Alice would understand the reference to married life, as things like this are normally kept hidden from children, however by referring to this in the poem Carroll undermines the seriousness of all the things children are brought up to value. What is also significant in this instance is the Caterpillar's response to Alice's recitation:

> 'That is not said right,' said the Caterpillar.
> 'Not quite right, I'm afraid,' said Alice timidly: 'Some of the words have got altered.'
> 'It is wrong from beginning to end,' said the Caterpillar, decidedly; and there was silence for some minutes.
>
> (AA. p.45)

He doesn't claim that Alice personally has altered the poem; just that it was not 'said' right. Alice similarly omits any direct reference to herself claiming that some of the words 'got altered', rather than 'were altered' (by herself). As is described by Jean-Jacques Lecercle (1994) during her recital of the poem Alice is reduced to the state of a tape player, saying words that are not her own.[19] The suggestive of this is that we are all mere mouthpieces, relaying information that is not our own, that we don't understand, yet don't question.

Similar implications can be found in Chapter 3 of *Through the Looking Glass*, when Alice finds herself on the train and everybody speaks to her in chorus (AA. p.149), then 'to her [Alice's] great surprise, they all thought in chorus' (AA. p. 149). At this point, Carroll as the narrator brings himself into the story, commenting 'I hope you understand what *thinking in chorus* means – for I must confess that *I* don't' (AA. p. 149), which invites the reader to become active in their perception of the text. Smug narrow-mindedness was a well known quality associated with the Victorian era, therefore when analysed in this context the text is highly suggestive of the extension of the constraints of nineteenth century norms and values beyond social boundaries, influencing how people think.

Nobody questions anybody in Wonderland, everybody just accepts everything for what it is, and this is Carroll's reflection of Victorian society, a society in which mathematical, linguistic, and evolutionary theories were accepted as truth.

Chapter 2: How Carroll is Subversive and Satirizes Victorian Reality

Alice's inquisitive nature functions to make prominent this notion, as her behaviour is notably opposite to the remaining Wonderland inhabitants. During her encounter with the Duchess in *Alice's Adventures in Wonderland* Alice voices her inability to accept one of the Duchess' claims:

> 'Very true,' said the Duchess: 'flamingoes and mustard both bite. And the moral of that is – "Birds of a fleather flock together."'
> 'Only mustard isn't a bird,' Alice remarked.
>
> (AA. p. 80)

The Duchess becomes frustrated by Alice's questioning tone, and further on in the conversation remarks:

> 'Thinking again?' the Duchess asked, with another dig of her sharp little chin.
> 'I've got a right to think,' said Alice sharply, for she was beginning to feel a little worried.
> 'Just about as much right,' said the Duchess, 'as pigs have to fly; and the m – '
>
> (AA. p. 81)

Therefore by making prominent the naïve nature of the Wonderland creatures towards even the most ridiculous notions, Carroll is not only satirising the inventors of such theories, but also a society that encourages and allows such nonsense to exist. As observed by the character of Humpty Dumpty about Alice, 'you're so exactly like other people' (AA. p. 166). Although he goes on to indicate physical characteristics, the initial implication is that individual difference is not accounted for within Victorian society, neither through education, culture, language or beliefs. The layman's assumption that common meanings in language use are known and clear, therefore the lack of tolerance towards other cultures that exists within nineteenth century society, is discussed further in Chapter 4.

In Chapter 6 of *Alice's Adventures in Wonderland* Alice enters a house, and what greets her can only be described as an unthinkable scene in Victorian England:

> The door led right into a large kitchen, which was full of smoke from one end to the other: the Duchess was sitting on a three-legged stool in the middle, nursing a baby: the cook was

Chapter 2: How Carroll is Subversive and Satirizes Victorian Reality

leaning over the fire, stirring a large cauldron which seemed to be full of soup.

(AA. pp. 52-53)

The nonsense becomes even more so, when the 'the cook...set to work throwing everything within her reach at the Duchess and the baby' (AA. p. 53). The Duchess is the highest titled rank of nobility in Victorian England, therefore for her to be in a kitchen, nursing a baby while being abused by her employee is a shocking display and violation of Victorian conduct and the social order. Therefore Carroll is highly subversive in portraying such an image.

However, at the opposite end of the spectrum, Jackie Wullschlager (1995) acknowledges Stanley Weintraub's biography of Queen Victoria as highly suggestive of how *parallel* Carroll's fantasy is to Victorian reality. Weintraub takes the Queen of Heart's statement, 'I don't know what you mean by *your* way. All the ways round here belong to me' (AA. p. 142), as an epigraph of Victoria:

Some scenes from Victoria's life read as they though they come from the Alice books. Ceremonial dinners, for example, were cleared away, while guests were still eating, the instant the Queen, who was served first and ate fast, had finished her portion, leaving visiting aristocrats hungry and humiliated. When arguments were not going her way, Victoria flirted with madness, clutching her head and crying 'my reason! my reason!' The Queen was haughtily remote from her subjects, never read a newspaper, opposed reform, and rigorously supported social hierarchies. [20]

Carroll's representation of The Queen of Hearts in *Alice's Adventures in Wonderland* was the embodiment of her autocratic and fanciful behavior. Carroll paints a similar portrait in *Through the Looking Glass*, for example when the Red Queen orders Alice to 'open your mouth a little wider when you speak, and always say "your majesty."' (AA. p. 142), and at the dinner party in Chapter 9 when the Red Queen persistently orders the food to be removed from the table and for the next course to be bought along before any of the guests have time to eat:

Chapter 2: How Carroll is Subversive and Satirizes Victorian Reality

'But the Red Queen looked sulky, and growled 'Pudding – Alice: Alice – Pudding: Remove the pudding!', and the waiters took it away so quickly that Alice couldn't return its bow.

(AA. p. 235)

However, Carroll's life indicates his fervent admiration of the Queen. He was a clergyman ordained in the Church of England, an Oxford academic, and conformed to the prevailing customs of society – on one occasion he wrote to *The Times* to complain about the irreverence displayed towards curates in a W.S. Gilbert play.[21] Yet his conformist lifestyle made him an intense loner who the restraint of nineteenth century society pushed into real eccentricity. The fact that he was a man of the Church made the Alice books extremely subversive, especially since the main character was a Victorian girl who should be an embodiment of politeness and good behaviour. Alice frequently ruins such values whilst in Wonderland. She ignored the The Fish-Footman's order not to enter the house, deeming him 'perfectly idiotic!' as she did so (AA. p. 52), then she indignantly sat down to the Mad Hatter's tea party even though all the other occupants cried

'No room! No room!' when she entered (AA. p. 60). Even more bold so, she challenges the Queen's order in the courtroom of 'Sentence first – vedict afterwards', loudly remarking 'Stuff and nonsense!...The idea of having the sentence first! (AA. p. 108). Such behaviour can be reasoned by the fact that the conventions of politeness Alice adheres to in Wonderland are turned against her. For example when she politely asks the King 'I beg your pardon' and he abruptly replies 'It isn't respectable to beg (AA. p. 200). If we look at how Alice addressed the Caterpillar at the very beginning of her adventures she *is* the embodiment of politeness:

> 'Who are you?'
> Alice replied, rather shyly, 'I – I hardly know, Sir, just at present - ...'
>
> (AA. p. 40)

As is noted by Jean-Jacques Lecercle (1994), whilst the characters in Wonderland constantly appeal to the notion of 'good manners' and remind Alice that she must be on her politest behaviour when in conversation with others, they rarely conform to the maxims of politeness themselves.[22] Examples of such include the derogatory remarks of the Caterpillar to Alice early on in *Alice's Adventures in Wonderland* in spite of her mannerly behaviour towards him: "You!" said the Caterpillar contemptuously. "Who are *you*?"', the abuse of the Sheep who deems her 'a little goose' in *Through the Looking Glass*, the Duchess's criticism of "You don't know much...and that's a fact". When the Hatter cuts off Alice mid-sentence 'this piece of rudeness was more than Alice could bear: she got up in great disgust, and walked off' (AA. p. 67). Even when addressing each other the creatures of Wonderland are just as rude. During the game of croquet in *Alice's Adventures in Wonderland* 'there was a dispute going on between the executioner, the King, and the Queen, who were all talking at once' (AA. p. 76):

> ...the moment Alice appeared, she was appealed to by all three to settle the question and they repeated their arguments to her, though, as they all spoke at once, she found it very hard to make out exactly what they said.
> (AA. pp. 76-77)

In this instance it is made clear that the conversation is not waged by the rules of politeness, language is used as a weapon to defeat ones opponent, rather than as a means of co-operation. (Lecercle, Jean Jacques, 1990)

'Except for 'God', the most popular word in the Victorian vocabulary must have been work''. [23] Therefore Carroll satires Victorian reality further by promoting the theme of play within the Alice books particularly through the 'White Knight's song'. As has already being discussed, a technique of Carroll's is to re-invent well known nursery rhymes and poems, and as is located by Judge Edward Abbot Parry, in this instance the poem is an obvious parody of Wordsworth's *Resolution of Independence*.[24] Alice's reaction 'But the tune isn't his own invention' (AA. p. 219) calls on the reader to recognise this re-invention and compare the two poems. Both poems pose the question 'And how is it you live?' to an old man. Referring to God, Wordsworth asks:

> But how can He expect that others should
> Build for him, sow for him, and at his call
> Love him, who for himself will take no heed at all?

Chapter 2: How Carroll is Subversive and Satirizes Victorian Reality

He finds an answer to this question in the old Man, who gave him 'human strength, by apt admonishment'. The old Man 'perseveres', which as is discussed by Kathleen Blake (1974) means metaphysically that he approaches life not as play but as earnest duty and endurance.[25] Wordsworth finds the 'longing comfort' he had been looking for in the old Man, who 'roamed, from moor to moor; Housing, with God's good help' and gathering leeches to earn a living. The poem ends with him describing how:

> I could have laughed myself to scorn to find
> In that decrepit Man so firm a mind.
> "God," said I, "be my help and stay secure;
> I'll think of the Leech-gatherer on the lonely moor!"

Blake (1974) points out what a 'Strange Comfort!' this is, and discusses further how Wordsworth stands admonished to abandon the carefree lifestyle defined by the speaker of the poem, who describes how 'My whole life I have lived in pleasant thought / As if life's business were a summer mood', and resign himself to the more religiously sanctioned duty of work. The aged Man in the White Knight's song has an attitude parallel to that of the old Man in *Resolution and Independence*, he perseveres and approaches life as earnest duty and endurance:

> "I sometimes dig for buttered rolls,
> Or set limed twigs for crabs:
> I sometimes search the grassy knolls
> For wheels of Hansom-cabs.
> And that's the way" (he gave a wink)
> "By which I get my wealth –
> And very gladly will I drink
> Your Honour's noble health."
>
> (AA. p. 221)

However, the White Knight's reaction to the virtues of the aged man, turn the conclusion that is implied by Wordsworth inside out. The circumstances that remind the White Knight are as Blake (1974) describes those that 'concern absentminded ineptness' [26]:

> And now, if e'er by chance I put
> My fingers into glue,
> Or madly squeeze a right-hand foot

Chapter 2: How Carroll is Subversive and Satirizes Victorian Reality

Into a left-hand shoe,
Or I drop upon my toe
A very heavy weight,
I weep, for it reminds me so
Of that old man I used to know –

(p. 221)

In this instance, Carroll 'throws into questions a valuation which would place work higher than play',[27] therefore satirizes Victorian values.

Chapter 3: Carroll's Issue

The *Alice* books are full of games and riddles. As with the 'White Knight's Song', many critics have perceived and upheld the implication of this to be that children need the freedom to play and to experiment, rather than strict discipline and education, therefore satirizing Victorian reality. However:

> 'the world Alice enters does not operate according to mental structures of an age younger than herself – an innocent flamboyant realm of presocialized freedom and un-rule bound self-expression. If this were the case the creatures would not be so insistent on her submission to their games. Rather this world represents an older level of mental organisation, characterized by an addiction to games with rules, with which Alice is expected to play along.' [28]

Free choice is essential to the play spirit; therefore the *Alice* stories are not representative of a world in which children are given the freedom to play. But the games and riddles encountered by Alice throughout her adventures in Wonderland are indeed part of the satire, as it is further suggestive of a reality in which people are expected to follow rules and laws that are sometimes impossible to comprehend. As is suggested by T.E. Hulme, Alice's dilemma in Wonderland is that 'A line...seems about to unite the whole word logically. But the line stops. There is no unity. All logic and life are made up of tangled ends like that.'[29] This is precisely Carroll's issue.

'Why is a raven like a writing-desk?' (AA. p.60) is a riddle made famous through the Alice books. Alice was asked the riddle by the Mad Hatter during the tea-party in Chapter 7 of *Alice's Adventures in Wonderland*. The interest it provoked is generated by the fact that no hint of an answer to it is given in the text:

> 'Have you guessed the riddle yet?' the Hatter said, turning to Alice again.
> 'No, I give it up,' Alice replied. 'What's the answer?'
> 'I haven't the slightest idea,' said the Hatter.
> 'Nor I,' said the March Hare.
> (AA. pp. 62-63)

Chapter 3: Carroll's Issue

As is noted by Edward Wakeling (1995); in the original version of the 'Preface to the Eighty-Sixth Thousand" in *Alice's Adventures in Wonderland*, Carroll gives this statement:

> Enquires have been so often addressed to me, as to whether any answer to the Hatter's riddle...can be imagined, that I may as well put on record here what seems to me to be a fairly appropriate answer, viz. "Because it can produce a few notes, though they are *very* flat; and it is never put with the wrong end in front!" This, however, is merely an afterthough: the Riddle, as originally invented, had no answer at all. [30]

If this is the case then 'Carroll himself was certainly teasing Alice [and the reader] in this passage'.[31] Alice feels that the Hatter is wasting time 'asking riddles that have no answers' (AA. p. 63), therefore it can be interpreted that Carroll is parodying a society that wastes time inventing new things, teasing its inhabitants with the prospect of new theories that give no plausible answers.

Alice's Adventures in Wonderland and Through the Looking Glass: A Victorian Satire?

Alice's Adventures in Wonderland is based on a pack of cards, while the adventure she embarks on in *Through the Looking Glass* takes on the form of a game of chess, as is acknowledged by Alice herself: 'It's a great huge game of chess that's being played – all over the world – if this *is* the world at all, you know. Oh, what fun it is!' (AA. p. 144). Although there is a strict hierarchy in essence, the book exposes how everything does not fit into one or two inclusive systems. For example, while a King is of higher status than a Queen in a pack of cards, within *Alice in Wonderland* the Queen is the more dominate partner of the two:

> The Queen had only one way of settling all differences, great or small. 'Off with his head!' she said without even looking round.
> 'I'll fetch the executioner myself,' said the King eagerly, and he hurried off.
>
> (AA. p. 76)

Also, in spite of the Queen's high status within the pack of cards, her frequent demands to have somebody executed are never actually carried out, and the abuse of the Duchess by her employer

Chapter 3: Carroll's Issue

which has already being discussed rejects any social order.

In *Through the Looking Glass*, the Red and White Knight's battle to win Alice is absurd in the context of a chess game:

> 'She's *my* prisoner, you know!' the Red Knight said at last.
> 'Yes but then *I* came and rescued her!' the White Knight replied.
> 'Well, we must fight for her, then,' said the Red Knight, as he took up his helmet (which hung from the saddle, and was something the shape of a horse's head) and put it on.
> 'You will observe the Rules of Battle, of course?' the White Knight remarked, putting on his helmet too.
> 'I always do, and they began banging at each other with such fury that Alice got behind a tree to be out of the way of the blows.
>
> (AA. p. 209-210)

The fact that Alice is able to become a Queen also ignores the hierarchy of the chess board, as there can be no more than two Queens in a game of chess:

'But how *can* it have got there without my knowing it?' she said to herself, as she lifted it off, and set it on her lap to make out what it could possibly be.

It was a golden crown.

(AA. p. 223)

Alice herself observes the lack of logic with regards to the game:

Everything was happening so oddly that she didn't feel a bit surprised at finding the Red Queen and the White Queen sitting close to her, one on each side: she would have liked very much to ask them how they came there, but she feared it would not be quite civil.

(AA. p. 224)

The world Alice enters has no coherence; she bounds from the multiple and shifting universes that exist within Wonderland, being sucked into every game that she stumbles on. The lack of consistency that is imposed on Alice becomes unsettling to her:

'It was much pleasanter at home,' thought poor Alice, 'when one wasn't always growing larger and smaller, and being ordered about by mice and rabbits. I almost wish I hadn't gone down that rabbit-hole – '

(AA. p. 33)

As is discussed by W.H. Auden:

...according to Lewis Carroll, what a child desires before anything else is that the world in which he finds himself should make sense. It is not the commands and prohibitions, as such, which adults impose that he resents, but rather than he cannot perceive any law linking one command to another. [32]

The lack of consistency within nineteenth century values is mimicked and mocked through the *Alice* books. As is suggested by Jackie Wullschlager (1995), the prehistoric menagerie encountered by Alice as part of her initial experience in Wonderland is suggestive of the excitement and fear caused by the new theories of evolution featured in the Oxford debate of 1860, while the baby changing into a pig and the duchess becoming a sheep are humorously symbolic of the evolutionary theory of Charles Darwin.[33] Evolution is anti-Christian and the underlying conflict between evolution and Christianity is part of the inconsistency of nineteenth century values that is expressed by Carroll through the nonsense of the *Alice* books. 'God' was probably the most popular and widely used word in the Victorian, therefore it doesn't makes sense for society to value religion yet welcome and promote theories of evolution, as one contradicts the other. This is one of the tangled ends in life that Carroll can't make sense of. Across the political spectrum of the nineteenth century followers of the popular philosophy known as social Darwinism claimed the 'Survival of the fittest' concept, often confusing it to mean survival of the 'strongest', 'most advanced' or even 'most moral'. However the concept referred to the ability to fit in with a habitation environment, rather than actual physical ability. Through the *Alice* books, Carroll mimics the incomprehension of such concepts by many groups within Victorian society, by allowing such an approach to exist in Wonderland. Alice uses a 'survival of the strongest' approach to dominate the courtroom and knock down the jury in *Alice's Adventures in Wonderland*, and again to escape the chaos of the dinner party in *Through the Looking Glass*.

As is discussed by Jackie Wullschlager (1995), 'it is not hard to see in Alice a comic, nonsense version of the Victorian Everyman, bewildered by change, tormented by religious doubt, [and] terrified of an empty, godless cosmos'.[34] Alice's conversation with the Caterpillar when she claims that she can't explain herself 'because I'm not myself you see' (AA. p. 41) represents a loss of identity. Whilst her conversation with the Cheshire Cat implies a loss of direction:

> 'Would you tell me please, which way I ought to go from here?'
> 'That depends a good deal on where you want to get to,' said the Cat.
> 'I don't much care where – ' said Alice.
> 'Then it doesn't matter which way you go,' said the Cat.
> ' – so long as I get *somewhere*', Alice added as an explanation.

'Oh, you're sure to do that,' said the Cat, 'if you only walk long enough.'

(AA. p. 57)

Both of the Alice books end with Alice rejecting the chaos of Wonderland. In *Alice's Adventures in Wonderland* this happens during the courtroom scene when the Knave of Hearts is been held trial for stealing the Queen of Heart's tarts and Alice is called to the stand to give evidence. Before the jury have time to consider their verdict the Queen exclaims 'No, No!...Sentence first – verdict afterwards.' (AA. p. 108). Alice, who at this point has grown so tall that she appeared to stand 'Nearly two miles high' (AA. p. 105) to the other Wonderland creatures, becomes infuriated with such nonsense and ends up in a 'survival of the strongest' row with the Queen:

'Stuff and nonsense!' said Alice loudly. 'The idea of having the sentence first!'
'Hold your tongue!' said the Queen, turning purple.
'I won't!' said Alice.
'Off with her head!' The Queen shouted at the top of her voice. Nobody moved.

Chapter 3: Carroll's Issue

'Who cares for *you?*' said Alice (she had grown to her full size by this time). 'You're nothing but a pack of cards!'
At this the whole pack rose up into the air, and came flying down upon her; she gave a little scream, half of fright and half of anger, and tried to beat them off...'

(AA. p. 108-9)

Through the Looking Glass ends with a similar rage at Alice's dinner party to celebrate her becoming a Queen:

The candles all grew up to the ceiling, looking something like a bed of rushes with fireworks at the top. As to the bottles, they each took a pair of plates, which they hastily fitted on as wings, and so, with forks for legs, went fluttering about in all directions.

(AA. p. 237)

The White Queen had gone and in it's place 'there was the leg of mutton sitting in the chair...and the soup-ladle was walking up the table towards Alice...beckoning to her impatiently to get out of its way' (AA. p. 237). Alice was once again infuriated by such nonsense, crying out 'I can't stand this any longer!', to with which she seized up the tablecloth crashing down everything on it, including the guests, to a heap on the floor. Her attack on the Red Queen, who 'had suddenly dwindled down to the size of a little doll' (AA. p. 239), was even fiercer:

> 'As for *you*,' she repeated, catching hold of the little creature in the very act of jumping over a bottle which had just lighted upon the table, "I'll shake you into a kitten, that I will!'
> She shook her off the table as she spoke, and shook her backwards and forwards with all her might.
>
> (AA. pp.239-40)

Carroll instils an important message through such images, a message of rejection of the restraints of the nineteenth century. As is concluded by Jackie Wullschlager (1995): "In images of destruction, Carroll took revenge on a repressive society and on his own frustrations". She discusses further how the random violence (the Duchess in the kitchen scene; the Queen who wants to cut everybody's head off; Alice's behaviour in the courtroom and at the dinner table; the purposeless battle of Tweedledee and Tweedledum; the 'Speak Roughly to Your Little Boy' poem) builds up a picture of a mindless world whose only certainty is death.[35]

Chapter 4: Carroll's Use of Language

As with the law and norms of society, Carroll feels the constraints of nineteenth century language conventions, therefore he exploits the loopholes of grammar through the *Alice* books. However, unlike laws, rules can not only be exploited, but they can also be defeated.[36] Through the nonsensical conversations that Alice finds herself part of during her adventures in Wonderland, Carroll defeats the rules of language. Throughout the books use of language is brought forth to the reader's attention. An example given by Danuta Zadworna-Fjellstad (1996) is the discussion of 'Reeling and Writhing' lessons for creatures of the sea (AA. p. 86), whereby the reader 'is startled into noticing the play on words and concepts'.[37]

In *Alice's Adventures in Wonderland* Alice is asked the question 'Who are *you*?' by a Caterpillar she discovers sitting on top of a mushroom smoking a hoodkah. Amongst the nonsense of the events she has so far encountered in Wonderland (shrinking in size then growing again), Alice's existence has become somewhat of a confusion to her, therefore she struggles to answer such a question:

Alice replied, rather shyly, 'I – I hardly know, Sir, just at present – at least I know who I *was* when I got up this morning, but I think I must have been changed since then.'
'What do you mean by that?' said the Caterpillar, sternly. 'Explain yourself!'
'I can't explain myself, I'm afraid, Sir,' said Alice, 'because I'm not myself, you see.'
'I don't see,' said the Caterpillar.

(AA. p. 41)

Whilst Alice's notion that she can't explain herself because she is not herself, allows the question to take on new meaning – rather than interpreting the question's literal form to explain what she means by what she has said, she interprets it figuratively as meaning explain her personification, the caterpillar answers with 'a common sense so excessively literally that it threatens to subvert the generally accepted view it is supposed to express' – 'I don't see'.[38]

In Chapter 6 of *Through the Looking Glass* Alice encounters Humpty Dumpty, who has become an even more significant character in the book for subverting a commonsensical view of language:

'And only *one* for birthday presents, you know. There's glory for you!'

'I don't know what you mean by "glory,"' Alice said.

Humpty Dumpty smiled contemptuously. 'Of course you don't – till I tell you. I meant "there's a nice knock-down argument for you!"'

'But "glory" doesn't mean "a nice knock-down argument,"' Alice objected.

'When I use a word,' Humpty Dumpty said, in a rather scornful tone, 'it means just what I choose it to mean – neither more nor less.'

(AA. p. 190).

As is observed by Robert Sutherland (1970), Humpty Dumpty's theoretical position on the nature and function of words 'is...a proper protest against the pedantic grammarian' demand that we should always use our words in the same senses as Samuel Johnson or some other 'authority', and never in any sense not found in the *Oxford English Dictionary*'.[39] Humpty Dumpty is given credit for his view of language when it is decided by Alice that he seems 'very clever at explaining words' (AA. p. 191), and asks him "Would you kindly tell me the meaning of the poem called "Jabberwocky"?' (AA. p. 191). Jabberwocky is the poem that was read by a nosy Alice from the White King's 'enormous memorandum-book' (AA. p. 133) in Chapter 1 of *Through the Looking Glass*. It begins with this and continues like so for a further six verses:

'Twas brillig, and the slithy toves
  Did gyre and gimble in the wabe:
All mimsy were the borogoves,
And the mome raths outgrabe.

(AA. p. 134)

Humpty Dumpty defines the 'hard words' in the Jabberwocky poem with no difficulty. However, it seems that he is merely guessing at their meanings, and if this is the case then the character of Humpty Dumpty functions to mimic the conduct of literary critics and philosophers of the nineteenth century in a satirizing manner, who 'commited ludicrous etymological errors through ignorance of historical relationships of languages, through false analogies and hasty generalisations', and used outlandish jargon to justify such theories.[40] Carroll not only creates and defines absurd words through the character of Humpty

Dumpty, he actually provides the reader with a defining concept to explain and justify their function. When explaining the word *'slithy'* Humpty Dumpty adds: 'Well, "*slithy*" means "lithe and slimy." "Lithe" is the same as "active." You see it's like a portmanteau - there are two meanings packed into one word'. (AA. p. 192). Further on in the conversation when Humpty Dumpty is explaining the meaning of the word "*mimsy*" to Alice as a mixture of both the words "flimsy and miserable" (AA. p. 193), Carroll, as the narrator, enters the dialect and points out to the reader '(there's another portmanteau for you)' (AA. p. 193). The significance of partly justifying the practice of Humpty Dumpty is that Carroll suddenly becomes extremely subversive. In the preface to *The Hunting of the Snark* (1876) Carroll published a statement noting how 'Humpty Dumpty's theory of two meanings packed into one word like a portmanteau, seems to me the right explanation for all'. However, Jean-Jacques Lecercle (1994) points out how the reaction of many critics was that the 'insane' coinages of portmanteau words do not respect rules of any kind, especially those of syntax, and it goes further by mimicking the Victorian pre-occupation with the production of dictionaries.[41]

Alice's Adventures in Wonderland and Through the Looking Glass:
A Victorian Satire?

Carroll also exploits the inadequacy of language as a means of communication and the difficulty in distinguishing meaning amongst and even within cultures, through the various instances in the Alice books where the meaning of what is said is misinterpreted. During an encounter with the King in *Through the Looking Glass*, Alice doesn't understand something and responds 'I beg your pardon?', to which the King exclaims 'It isn't respectable to beg' (AA. p. 200). Humpty Dumpty demonstrates similar misunderstanding of the phrase with the milder response 'I'm not offended' (AA. p. 189). Alice herself also experiences confusion of meaning when in conversation with the 'foreign' Wonderland creatures, for example during this scene with the King when he eats some hay to revive himself from feeling faint:

> '…there's nothing like eating hay when you're faint,' he remarked to her as he munched away.
> 'I should think throwing cold water over you would be better,' Alice suggested: ' – or some sal-volatile.'
> 'I didn't say there was nothing *better*,' the King replied. 'I said there was nothing *like* it.' Which Alice did not venture to deny.
>
> (AA. p. 201).

Chapter 4: Carroll's Use of Language

And again when Humpty Dumpty enquires about her age:

> '...so here's a question for you, how old did you say you were?'
> Alice made a short calculation, and said 'Seven years and six months.'
> 'Wrong!' Humpty Dumpty exclaimed triumphantly. 'You never said a word like it!'
> 'I though you meant "How old *are* you?"' Alice explained.
> 'If I'd meant that, I'd have said it,' said Humpty Dumpty. Alice didn't want to begin another argument, so she said nothing.
>
> (AA. p. 188)

Humpty Dumpty's reaction is what is significant in this instance; he triumphs over the fact that Alice answers the question wrong, and his attitude can be defined as arrogant. This is similar to the old Sheep's reaction to Alice's incomprehension of the word 'Feather'. In Chapter 5 of *Through the Looking Glass* Alice finds herself in a little boat with the old Sheep, who keeps crying the word 'Feather!' to her. When Alice eventually enquires as to what the old sheep means by the word, not only does she fail to acknowledge the question of meaning, but deems Alice 'a little goose' for her lack of comprehension:

> 'Feather! Feather!' the Sheep cried again, taking more needles. 'You'll be catching a crab directly.'
> 'A dear little crab!' thought Alice. 'I should like that.'
> 'Didn't you hear me say "Feather"?' the Sheep cried angrily, taking up quite a bunch of needles.
> 'Indeed I did,' said Alice: 'you've said it very often – and very loud. Please where *are* the crabs?'
> 'In the water, of course!' said the Sheep, sticking some of the needles into her hair, as her hands were full. 'Feather, I say!'
> '*Why* do you say "Feather" so often?' Alice asked at last, rather vexed. 'I'm not a bird!'
> 'You are,' said the Sheep: 'you're a little goose.'
>
> (AA. p. 180)

The old Sheep is using the word 'feather' in a context that Alice is not familiar with, however

Chapter 4: Carroll's Use of Language

she doesn't define her meaning of the word to Alice, but simply expects her to know what she means and treats her with verbal abuse when she doesn't. As is expressed by Robert Sutherland (1970), this scene 'suggests a proper protest against the layman's assumption that common meanings are known and clear, and that there is some one 'correct' meaning for each word, in contrast to which all other meanings that may be given to it are 'incorrect'.[42] The old Sheep's inability to perceive that Alice may not have knowledge of the word's meaning is symbolic of the assumption that common meanings are known and clear, even to those unfamiliar with the English vocabulary.

During her encounter with Humpty Dumpty, Alice stumbles across another word that she doesn't understand however in this instance the Wonderland creature is much more helpful in defining the word to her:

> 'Would you tell me, please,' said Alice, 'what that means?'
> 'Now you talk like a reasonable child,' said Humpty Dumpty, looking very much pleased. 'I meant by "impenetrability" that we've had

enough of that subject, and it would be just as well if you'd mention what you mean to do next, as I suppose you don't mean to stop here all the rest of your life.'

'That's a great deal to make one word mean,' Alice said in a thoughtful tone.

(AA. p. 191)

Through Alice's reaction Carroll implies that 'a single word can embody too great a condensation of signification',[43] which again is suggestive of the failure of language as a mean to communicate. Her 'thoughtful tone' hints at the reader to also think about the notion that a word can perhaps signify too much. As has been discussed by Richard Robinson on this subject:

Most names, whether names of simple or of complex objects, fail to mirror by their structure any complexity in the object...To abbreviate a phrase into a word, therefore, is always to set up a cause that may lead men to overlook an important complexity or relation, or to find mystery where there is none. [44]

Chapter 4: Carroll's Use of Language

Referring back to the scene in which the mouse is telling a story actually borrowed from a history book to Alice and the other Wonderland creatures, the Duck raises a non-trivial linguistic question with regards to the meaning of the word 'it':

'Edward and Morcar, the earls of Mercia and Northumbia, declared for him; and even Stigan, the patriotic archbishop of Canterbury, found it advisable –'
'Found *what*?' said the Duck.
'Found *it*,' the Mouse replied rather crossly: 'of course you know what "it" means.'
'I know what "it" means well enough, when *I* find a thing' said the Duck: 'it's generally a frog or a worm. The question is, what did the archbishop find?
The mouse did not notice this question but hurriedly went on.

(AA. p.25)

By raising such a question Carroll is showing that, unlike contemporary grammarians, he is aware that there is a problem regarding the linguistic status of the word 'it', in terms of not deixis but anaphora, and implies that 'it' is anaphoric of a noun or noun phrase; 'this is where the cat is let out of Carroll's satirical bag'.[45] Jean-Jacques Lecercle (1990) discusses the failings of contemporary grammarians to be aware of such a problem, quoting the following from a Victorian grammar: 'When the infinitive is the nominative to a verb, it is often placed after it, and "it is" or some similar form introduces the sentence.' The example given is: 'It is impossible to make people understand their ignorance.' Lecercle goes on to explain how in the case when the infinitive is an object it is analysed as 'an appostion to "it"', as in 'he thought it best to go'. Such an analysis restricts the occurrence of 'it' to infinitives, and explains 'it' in terms of both 'insertion' and 'apposition', whereas nowadays the syntactic function of the infinitive is recognised as being only one grammatical phenomenon, susceptible of a single analysis.[46] By making the Duck ask the question, Carroll demonstrates his acute linguistic awareness and subverts and mocks the view of Victorian grammarians.

The trial scene in *Alice's Adventures in Wonderland* which takes up the last two chapters of the book is far more than a piece of satire. As is proposed by Jean-Jacques Lecercle (1994):

Chapter 4: Carroll's Use of Language

It is an account of the institutional violence of language, the power of rhetoric and sophistry, and of the necessity to agonistic retort if one does not wish to be made the victim of arbitrariness. [47]

Alice uses such a technique to produce sharp counterarguments to avoid the victimisation of her self and the other Wonderland creatures. This occurs initially when the King invents a rule to suit his own purposes, claiming that it is the law:

At this moment the King, who had been for some time busily writing in his note-book, called out 'Silence!', and read out from his book, 'Rule Forty-two. *All persons more than a mile high to leave the court.*'
Everybody looked at Alice.
'*I'm* not a mile high,' said Alice.
'You are,' said the King.
'Nearly two miles high,' added the Queen.
'Well, I shan't go, at any rate,' said Alice: 'besides, that's not a regular rule: you invented it just now.'
'It's the oldest rule in the book,' said the King.
'Then it ought to be Number One,' said Alice.

The King turned pale, and shut his note-book hastily. 'Consider your verdict,' he said to the jury, in a low trembling voice.

(AA. p. 105)

Alice's aggression and logical argument defeats the King, and she holds her stance in the courtroom. However her counterarguments are not always successful, and when she attempts to prevent the victimisation of the Knave of Hearts the King hardly registers her outburst:

> 'There's more evidence to come yet, please your Majesty,' said the White Rabbit, jumping up in a great hurry: 'this paper has just been picked up...it's a set of verses.'
> 'Are they in the prisoner's handwriting?' asked another of the jurymen.
> 'No, they're not,' said the White Rabbit, 'and that's the queerest thing about it.' (The jury all looked puzzled.)
> 'He must have imitated somebody else's hand,' said the King. (The jury all brightened up again.)

'Please your Majesty,' said the Knave, 'I didn't write it, and they can't prove that I did: there's no name signed at the end.'

'If you didn't sign it,' said the King, 'that only makes the matter worse. You *must* have meant some mischief, or else you'd have signed your name like an honest man.'

There was a general clapping of hands at this: it was the first really clever thing the King had said that day.

'That *proves* his guilt, of course,' said the Queen: 'so, off with - .'

'It doesn't even prove anything of the sort!' said Alice. 'Why, you don't even know what they're about.

'Read them,' said the King.

(AA. pp.105-106)

Although the Kings claims lack substantial justification, he is rhetorically cunning and in spite of Alice's public display of disagreement he has the jury believing that the letter is 'the most important piece of evidence we've heard yet (AA. p. 107). Lecercle re-tells how to break the spell Alice demonstrates an act of arbitrary violence, by exclaiming to the jury 'You're nothing but a pack of cards!' (AA. p. 109).[48]

Jean-Jacques Lecercle (1994) accurately sums up how through nonsense Carroll 'echoes, stages and intervenes upon the contradictions of language as both object and vehicle of Victorian pedagogy'.[49]

Conclusion

Finally, it must be asked, how valid is the apparently calculated adult background of *Alice* if it was evidently written for children and never intended to be published? As is discussed in the Introduction to the *Alice* books:

...most of Alice's Adventures in Wonderland was told spontaneously to three little girls and written down from memory for their private amusement, before being expanded for the larger audience of whom its author had no thought when telling or writing the original version. [50]

Alice herself recalls how it was she who 'started to pester him [Carroll] to write down the story',[51] and if the apparent deeper meaning that gives the fairytale an added dimension does exist, it cannot possibly of being understood by her or her sisters, therefore done for the benefit of the listener. However the suggestiveness of the text's structure cannot be argued, which implies that Lewis did it out of his own needs and longings, 'as a chance to reduce to chaos some of the establishment values –

the law ('Sentence first – verdict afterwards'), education (reeling and writhing) – which publicly he upheld'[52]; therefore to be enjoyed by himself as the story teller.

The use of language, the reference to and reinvention of well known sayings and nursery rhymes, the prominence of education and etiquette grouped with the linguistically self-reflexive narrating of the stories signal the deep social content of this text of nonsense. Whether or not Carroll intended the Alice books to be a public satire, out of the dark interiors of Victorian fantasy he created a satirizing social comedy about the norms and values of nineteenth century society. The incidents and characters in the book are so parallel to Victorian reality that this cannot be denied.

Notes

[1] C.S. Lewis, 'On Three Ways of Writing for Children', a lecture read to the Library Association and published in its *Proceedings*, (1952), quoted in the 'Introduction' to *Alice's Adventures in Wonderland and Through the Looking-Glass*, (1998), Oxford: Oxford University Press, p. ix

[2] Robinson Duckworth, *The Lewis Carroll Picture Book* ed. Stuart Dodgson Collingwood, (1899), T Fisher Unwin: London. pp. 359-60

[3] Lewis Carroll, 'Introduction' to *Alice Adventures in Wonderland and Through the Looking Glass*, (1998), Oxford: Oxford University Press. (p. xv)

[4] Archdeacon Charles Dodgson to Lewis Carroll, (1840), quoted in Derek Hudson, *Lewis Carroll, An Illustrated Biography*, new edition, (1976), Constable: London. p. 35

[5] Jackie Wullschlager, *Inventing Wonderland: The Lives and Fantasies of Lewis Carroll, Edward Lear, J.M. Barrie, Kenneth Grahame and A.A. Milne*, (1995), Methuen: London. p. 64

[6.] Letter from E. K. Jupp, Junior Student at Christchurch, to his brother (1868), quoted in Derek Hudson, *Lewis Carroll, An Illustrated Biography*, new edition, (1976), Constable: London. p. 131

[7.] Lewis Carroll, 'Alice on the Stage', *The Theatre*, April 1887, quoted in Jackie Wullschlager, *Inventing Wonderland: The Lives and Fantasies of Lewis Carroll, Edward Lear, J.M. Barrie, Kenneth Grahame and A.A. Milne*, (1995), Methuen: London. p. 48

[8.] Lewis Carroll, *Alice's Adventures in Wonderland and Through the Looking-Glass*, (1998), Oxford: Oxford University Press.
Further references to this work will be given in the text, abbreviated 'AA'.

[9.] Jackie Wullschlager. p. 50

[10.] Lewis Carroll to F. H. Atkinson, (10 December 1898), quoted in Jackie Wullschlager, *Inventing Wonderland: The Lives and Fantasies of Lewis Carroll, Edward Lear, J.M. Barrie, Kenneth Grahame and A.A. Milne*, (1995), Methuen: London. p. 58

[11] Jackie Wullschlager. p. 59

[12] Jackie Wullschlager. p. 59

[13] Abraham Ettleson, M.D., *Lewis Carroll's 'Through the Looking Glass' Decoded*, (1966), Philosophical Library: New York.

[14] Jean Jacques Lecercle, *Philosophy of Nonsense: The Intuitions of Victorian Nonsense Literature*, (1994), Routledge: London and New York. p. 195

[15] Jackie Wullschlager. p. 44

[16] Jackie Wullschlager. p. 41

[17] Linda Hutcheon, *Narcissistic Narrative: The Metafictional Paradox*, (1980), Wilfrid Laurier University Press: Ontario. pp.99-102

[18] Jean Jacques Lecercle, *Philosophy of Nonsense*. p. 217

[19] Jean Jacques Lecercle, *Philosophy of Nonsense*. p. 118

[20] Jackie Wullschlager. pp. 45-46

21. Jackie Wullschlager. pp. 46

22. Jean-Jacques Lecercle, *Philosophy of Nonsense*. p. 103

23. Walter E. Houghton, *The Victorian Frame of Mind'*, (1957), Oxford University Press: London. p. 242

24. Judge Edward Abbot Parry 'The Early Writings of Lewis Carroll', *Cornhill Magazine* (April 1924) p. 459-462, quoted in Kathleen Blake, *Play, Games, and Sport: The Literary Works of Lewis Carroll*, (1974), Cornell University Press: New York. pp. 95-96

25. Kathleen Blake, *Play, Games, and Sport: The Literary Works of Lewis Carroll*, (1974), Cornell University Press: New York. p.100

26. Kathleen Blake. p. 102

27. Kathleen Blake. p.104

28. Kathleen Blake. p.118

[29] Hulme, T. E., "Cinders" in *T. E. Hulme: Selected Writings edited with an introduction by Patrick McGuiness*, (2003), Routeldge: New York. p. 30

[30] Edward Wakeling, *Rediscovered Lewis Carroll Puzzles*, (1995), Dover Publications: New York. (p. 167)

[31] Francis Huxley, *The Raven and The Writing Desk*, (1976), Thames and Hudson: London. (p. 167)

[32] Auden, W. H., *Today's Wonder-World Needs Alice*, (July 1962), New York Times Magazine: New York. p.5, quoted in Kathleen Blake, *Play, Games, and Sport: The Literary Works of Lewis Carroll*, (1974), Cornell University Press: New York. p. 106

[33] Jackie Wullschlager. pp. 44-45

[34] Jackie Wullschlager. p. 50

[35] Jackie Wullschlager. pp. 50-52

[36] Robert D. Sutherland, *Language and Lewis Carroll*, (1970), Mouton & Co. N.V., Publishers: The Hague. p. 156

37. Danuta Zadworna-Fjellstad, *Alice's Adventures in Wonderland and Gravity's Rainbow: A Study in Duplex Fiction*, (1996), Minab/Gotab: Stockholm. p. 28

38. J. P. Brisset, *La Grammaire logique*, (1970), Tchou: Paris, quoted in Jean Jacques Lecercle, *Philosophy of Nonsense: The intuitions of Victorian nonsense literature*, (1994), Routledge: London and New York. p. 119

39. Richard Robinson, *Definition*, pp. 72-73, quoted in Robert D. Sutherland, *Language and Lewis Carroll*, (1970), Mouton & Co. N.V., Publishers: The Hague. pp. 157 - 158

40. Robert D. Sutherland. p. 149

41. Jean Jacques Lecercle, *Philosophy of Nonsense*. p. 23

42. Robinson, Richard, *Definition*, pp. 72-73, quoted in Robert D. Sutherland, *Language and Lewis Carroll*, (1970), Mouton & Co. N.V., Publishers: The Hague. pp. 157 - 158

43. Robert D. Sutherland. pp. 156-157

44. Robinson, Richard, *Definition*, p. 79, quoted in Robert D. Sutherland, *Language and Lewis Carroll*, (1970), Mouton & Co. N.V., Publishers: The Hague. p. 156

45. Jean Jacques Lecercle, *The Violence of Language*, (1990), Routledge: London and New York. p. 15

46. Jean Jacques Lecercle, *The Violence of Language*, pp. 15-16

47. Jean Jacques Lecercle, *Philosophy of Nonsense*, p. 90

48. Jean Jacques Lecercle, *Philosophy of Nonsense*, p. 90

49. Jean Jacques Lecercle, *Philosophy of Nonsense*, p. 220

50. Lewis Carroll, 'Introduction', *Alice Adventures in Wonderland and Through the Looking Glass*, (1998), Oxford: Oxford University Press. p. xi

51. 'Alice's Recollections of Carrollian Days, told to her son, Caryl Hargreaves', *Cornhill Magazine*, (July 1932), quoted in the 'Introduction' to *Alice's Adventures in Wonderland and Through the Looking-*

Glass, (1998), Oxford: Oxford University Press. p. xii

52. Jackie Wullschlager. pp. 46-47

Bibliography

Blake, Kathleen, *Play, Games, and Sport: The Literary Works of Lewis Carroll*, (1974), Cornell University Press: New York.

Carroll, Lewis, *Alice's Adventures in Wonderland and Through the Looking-Glass*, (1998), Oxford: Oxford University Press.

Duckworth, Robinson, *The Lewis Carroll Picture Book* ed. Stuart Dodgson Collingwood, (1899), T Fisher Unwin: London.

Ettleson, Abraham, M.D., *Lewis Carroll's 'Through the Looking Glass' Decoded*, (1966), Philosophical Library: New York.

Houghton, Walter, E., *The Victorian Frame of Mind'*, (1957), Oxford University Press: London.

Hudson, Derek, *Lewis Carroll, An Illustrated Biography*, new edition, (1976), Constable: London.

Hutcheon, Linda, *Narcissistic Narrative: The Metafictional Paradox*, (1980), Wilfrid Laurier University Press: Ontario.

Huxley, Francis, *The Raven and The Writing Desk*, (1976), Thames and Hudson: London.

Lecercle, Jean Jacques, *The Violence of Language*, (1990), Routledge: London and New York.

Lecercle, Jean-Jacques, *Philosophy of Nonsense: The intuitions of Victorian nonsense literature*, (1994), Routledge: London and New York.

Sutherland, Robert. D., *Language and Lewis Carroll*, (1970), Mouton & Co. N.V., Publishers: The Hague.

T. E. Hulme: *Selected Writings edited with an introduction by Patrick McGuiness*, (2003), Routeldge: New York.

Wakeling, Edward, *Rediscovered Lewis Carroll Puzzles*, (1995), Dover Publications: New York.

Wullschlager, Jackie, *Inventing Wonderland: The Lives and Fantasies of Lewis Carroll, Edward Lear, J.M. Barrie, Kenneth Grahame and A.A. Milne*, (1995), Methuan: London.

Zadworna-Fjellstad, Danuta, *Alice's Adventures in Wonderland and Gravity's Rainbow: A Study in Duplex Fiction*, (1996), Minab/Gotab: Stockholm.

www.ingramcontent.com/pod-product-compliance
Lightning Source LLC
Chambersburg PA
CBHW031644170426
43195CB00035B/574